POEMS, PRAYERS & PRAISE

Pieces of Me

JANET L. MONTGOMERY

WESTBOW
PRESS®
A DIVISION OF THOMAS NELSON
& ZONDERVAN

WestBow Press books may be ordered through booksellers or by contacting:

WestBow Press
A Division of Thomas Nelson & Zondervan
1663 Liberty Drive
Bloomington, IN 47403
www.westbowpress.com
844-714-3454

ISBN: 978-1-6642-9659-6 (sc)
ISBN: 978-1-6642-9660-2 (hc)
ISBN: 978-1-6642-9658-9 (e)

Library of Congress Control Number: 2023906201

Print information available on the last page.

WestBow Press rev. date: 05/26/2023

In loving memory
of
Shaunte Cephus
My pastor and friend

Until we meet Again …
Thank You.

Shaunte Cephus
August 29, 1978–October 2, 2022
Pastor, Epic Encounters Church
San Diego, CA

CONTENTS

ACKNOWLEDGMENTS

It would be remiss of me not to acknowledge my pastor's role in helping with this book's creation. Shaunte Cephus was an anointed man of God and a blessing to my family. Shaunte preached holiness of the heart and was a great leader and friend. He was also a fisher of men, and when my family went through a hard time, he reached out to us regularly. Later, he would become our pastor and a close friend to my husband. Under Pastor Cephus's ministry, my husband would become a stronger minister and preacher of the gospel.

I loved Shaunte's appreciation and fascination with the spoken word. He enjoyed hip-hop and rap music for the lyrical poetry. He would often ask me to have poetry ready on Sundays. Sometimes it was hard because although I believed God inspired me to write poetry, sometimes, being the person who delivered these thoughts was difficult for me.

But ever the believer in the ministry of the spoken word, Shaunte made sure I had fresh material. It became a natural progression because I would run out of material and find it necessary to give fresh thoughts through poetry. So this would keep me busy and ready to share something new. This is how many of the poems in this collection came into existence.

So thank you, Pastor Shaunte, for keeping my pen busy these last few years. You believed in me when I didn't believe in myself. For this, I will always be grateful to you. You were a wonderful man of God that loved everyone. You broke down racial barriers and allowed God to use you in such a great way that we have to acknowledge you as the GOAT (Greatest of All Time) pastor to our church and to the numerous souls you've touched through your ministry in your short time with us. We will forever look to your example of what ministry for the Lord should be.

INTRODUCTION

Where does one begin when putting together their life story through poetry? I suppose I have hesitated all these years because I didn't like the thought of exposing some of the darker moments in my life. Yet release came through writing and with it, freedom from what people thought of me. Reality seemed to have a way of being expressed through my poetry, sometimes, a reality I wasn't ready to face. So I now share these expressions with those willing to turn the pages and see a darker side of a soul searching for truth and how God can come into the picture and bring healing.

At seventeen years old, I pondered the deeper things of life through poetry. This was when I wrote, "Promises Never Kept." An honest evaluation of what I thought my life had become. A product of a broken marriage, I was confused as to why things fell apart in my home. At the age of ten, my mother and father divorced, thus that broken promise would be the first of many to affect my life.

My personal walk with Christ also began at seventeen years old. I started what would result in a lifelong journey to a more personal relationship with Him. I started going to church to find myself. But somewhere along the way, I lost myself in trying to feel the acceptance of a very conservative church. I had to reevaluate my life and realize that God was calling me to a relationship with Him, and my purpose would need to be in serving Him and fulfilling His will in my life. Sometimes this meant walking away from things that hindered my relationship with Him. I have been a member of different churches, and recently, I have been praying for direction after the loss of my pastor. I believe in the church experience and look forward to congregating again, but as I have prayed for direction, I felt it was time to put this book together. After all these years, my church experience has brought me to a place where I felt it was time to share this poetry collection.

So thus begins this process for me, as always, putting pen to paper and finding out that God meant for this to be. I pray that some of these poems will touch you so that you, too, can know this great God who carries us through "the valley of the shadow of death." He can heal all of the pain of the past and give you a new reason to love the future. Allow him to speak to you through these *Poems, Prayers, and Praise* so that you too can understand that He loves you so much and still speaks to us today. He can speak to you through these poems if you let Him.

I

FAITH AND PRAYER

But without faith, it is impossible the please Him, for
he who comes to God must believe that He is and that
He is a rewarder of those who diligently seek Him.

—HEBREWS 11:6

The first step in having a relationship with God is faith. After forty years of living out my personal relationship with the Lord, I believe this. If you asked me what has been the most crucial aspect of my relationship with God, faith would have to be. Faith that He hears my prayers, that He cares, and that He is still listening. The next step to having a relationship with God is prayer. What is prayer but speaking to a heavenly Father who cares for you? This is where faith comes in; some of us have never encountered the unconditional love of a parent, much less the love of God, so it is hard to fathom the love of God. How does God speak to us? His Word gives us a glimpse of who He is; we may not understand the Bible, but if we learn how to pray and ask God for direction, He will answer our prayers. How does He lead us? Sometimes it is a still, small voice, and sometimes it's a dream or another manifestation or sign. But mostly, God will speak to us through His Word, the Bible.

Many of my poems came from longing to know God for myself. As you read this collection of poetry, I pray that you will allow God to speak to you and bring you a better knowledge of Him. He will hear your prayer and answer as you seek Him for yourself. You will find that He was closer than you realized. The journey of faith starts with a little prayer; for me, it was "God, if You are real, please show me." I began my life as a Buddhist, so I had no biblical teaching up to this point, but much of this poetry is based on scripture. That prayer began a spiritual awakening in my life that has continued to this day. I was seventeen when I wrote a poem called "Promises Never Kept"; until that time, I had been hurt so deeply by life that I had lost faith in everything and everyone. I realized that God was reaching out to me in my emptiness. So I begin this book with a look back into those years when it all started. A few months after writing this sad poem, I started taking my first steps to find God. There were only the first two stanzas in this poem until I recently finished this poem. I thank God for giving me that happier ending to my poem and life.

One of my favorite scriptures, one that I use as a pattern of prayer, is that of David in Psalm 61. If I had to recommend a scripture to anyone who is seeking God, this prayer would be what I would recommend. It is so powerful because it breaks down a prayer to the point of desperation: "When my heart is overwhelmed, lead me to the rock that is higher than

I." Sometimes we don't know the answers, and we need to ask for help. I found that the only way to know the Savior would be to devote daily time to seek Him. This started a prayer journey that led me to write about where I was in my life through journaling, as well as writing poetry. I thank God for inspiring me to share my poetry and prayers with you, and I pray they will help you in your own journey to know Him.

I recently added the last two stanzas for "Promises Never Kept." I felt like it didn't give a complete story, because God has made such a difference in my life since this was originally written when I was a teenager. God has been a heavenly Father who has provided my life with stability since those teen years. If there is any glory or any praise for what gifts I might have, it belongs to Him, but I believe it is time to share this poetry outside of church congregations and in a world that needs to hear a message of hope.

PROMISES NEVER KEPT

Promises never kept.
From pain, I'm never free.
If life was meant for living,
It wasn't meant for me.

How can you pick up the pieces
When there are no more pieces left
Of a life that is just bad memories
Of promises never kept?

Lord, pick up the pieces,
Those pieces left of me,
Those parts of me so broken
That no one else can see.

As I look beyond the pale
To a life that I once knew,
The love that never failed
Was only found in You.

PRAYER OF FAITH

....

You can wish … or
You can pray.
God hears you;
He knows your heart.
Faith is a substance.
Do you have it?
God is able.
Embrace His goodness
In the land of the living.
Express your faith
To a living God
Who answers prayer.
Put it in God's hands.
Trust in Him.
The everlasting arms
Will never fail you.
The everlasting Father
Will provide.
Faith is the answer,
The evidence
Of things not seen.
Open your eyes to see
Your miracle
With a prayer of faith.

LILY OF THE VALLEY

In everything, I give You thanks:
For good days and for bad,
For days I wished would end,
For dark and lonely valleys,
For the mountaintops,
For helping me understand
Life is a journey.

Thank You for the struggle,
For trials that made me strong,
For making me realize
I was never alone in that valley,
For answering my prayers,
For speaking quietly
Into a dark night of despair.

Thank You for this valley.
With it comes a revelation:
I can trust You to see me through
Every trial and test.
Most of all, thank You, Lord,
For being the Lily of the Valley,
For shining your love on me
And being the light in my darkness.

JUST A PRAYER AWAY

Just in case you ever wonder
When you look into the sky
If there's a God in heaven
Who hears each time you cry.

Just in case you ever look back
On days just like today
And wonder if He heard
That simple prayer you prayed.

The blessings of a Father,
The hope of better days,
All of this and more
Belong to those who pray.

Open up your heart.
Change your world today.
You just might find the answer
Is just a prayer away.

ONLY JESUS

Religious experience
Without knowing the Savior
In your own life
Will always leave you …
Empty.
Rules without relationship,
Programs and rituals,
Talking about the Savior
But not to the Savior
Is still missing it.
The plan of God
Is to worship Him
In spirit and truth.
So today
Let go of your past
And focus—
Not on a person
Or a program
Or a church—
Only Jesus.

THE CHOICE

Light has come
To a dark place.
What will you embrace?

When the Spirit of Christ
Speaks to your soul,
Will you hear His voice?

The love of God is greater
Than anything
Or anyone.
What can separate us
From His love?

Only ourselves.
Break the curse.
Choose light.
Choose life.
Choose Him.

LORD, HELP ME TO PRAY

When life comes crashing down
And no help can be found,
When hope seems far away,
In Your name, I will pray.
For every prayer, You hear.
Oh Lord, You are so near.
You're never far away.
So Lord, help me to pray.

Lord, I want to be like You
In everything I do.
And when life isn't fair,
I know that You still care
And You will see me through
Just like You always do.
You're never far away,
So Lord, help me to pray.

A SIMPLE PRAYER

If we only knew
How God waits
As we exhaust
Every resource.
But the secret
Was always
In a simple prayer:
Lord, help us to know
That You are with us,
To trust You,
To believe
You are working all things
Together for our good.
Lord, I trust You.
Change my life today
Through
A simple prayer.

SILENCE

In the silence
I will listen
For the still, small voice
That leads me on
Through the valleys
And mountain tops
I will praise Him.
For in the silence
I hear His voice
A voice of love,
With tender mercy
Calling me
To a place unknown.
But I shall know
His goodness
In the land of the living
Because He has called me,
Away from the noise
To hear his voice
In the silence

II

EVERLASTING FATHER

*For unto us a child is born, unto us, a son is given,
and the government will be upon His shoulder. And
His name will be called Wonderful, Counselor, Mighty
God, Everlasting Father, Prince of Peace.*

—ISAIAH 9:6

This is my favorite Christmas scripture in the Bible, not only for the poetic beauty of this prophecy given by the prophet Isaiah, who lived about seven hundred years before the birth of Christ, but because it gives the five names of God that speak of who He has been to me. My father was in the military, and I didn't see him very much growing up. When he retired, my mom and dad divorced shortly afterward. My father was an alcoholic. As much as I don't like talking about it, I have to admit there was an emptiness in me that I tried to fill because of it. I do have good memories of my father when I was younger, when things were better at home. But by the time I was ten, my father and mother divorced, and it was due to his infidelity. It was an ugly situation that I tried to escape by developing my own vices.

Having a relationship with God has been harder for me in the sense that much of the foundation and trust in my life was destroyed by the time I was a teenager. Relating to God as a heavenly Father would have to be a process that developed over many years. God has always been that heavenly Father who understood me in spite of my lack of faith. But much of my struggles with depression over the years came out of a lack of understanding and connection to God as my heavenly Father. But in moments of clarity, I can understand God's love and realize that my life may not have a strong connection to a natural father, but God has been a real Father in every sense of the word.

I have written a lot of poetry in my efforts to relate to a heavenly Father who loves me. I pray that you realize as you read these poems that God loves you more than your earthly father ever could. God created us, but we are not perfect and have our failures. My father was a good man but had many failures. As you realize you have a heavenly father, there is peace in knowing that He will never let you down.

I am thankful for the years that I did have a father; many people have never even known that. My father's kidneys failed, and he passed from this life at sixty-one. There were many medical complications prior to that, which made him unable to enjoy life; he had a stroke during this time and deteriorated mentally and physically afterward. I've said all of this to emphasize that our earthly fathers, no matter how wonderful or *not*, will not always be there for us. For many reasons, many fathers didn't even know how to parent, much less offer the stability and love that we, as children, so desperately need.

God is an *everlasting Father,* a Father when we are *fatherless.* Psychologically, spiritually, and even physically, our natural fathers will fail us because they are human, but God's love never fails us. None of us deserve His love, but it is as real now as when He gave His life on the cross. We may not understand why this was the plan for redemption, but it leaves little room to doubt the lengths God would go to reestablish that connection to us as our Father.

THE EVERLASTING FATHER

How do you express
To a father you have not known
The emptiness of longing
For a relationship with him?
How do you recover
From that emptiness?

The everlasting Father
Is calling to your soul.
Come and know the One
Who loves you more
Than mere words express.
Come and find hope
In your emptiness.
Come and know the Father
Of the fatherless.

Reach out to Him
As He reaches to you
In the quietness of night.
In the morning light,
You can hear His voice
Gently speak to your soul …

"I am the everlasting Father.
The One who covers you
In blood divine
So you can be reborn
From the ashes of your life.
Come unto Me,
And I will give you rest

From the longing of your soul,
From your emptiness.
Come unto Me,
And you will know
The everlasting Father."

Furthermore, we have had human fathers who corrected us, and we paid them respect. Shall we much more readily be in subjection to the father of Spirits and live? (Hebrews 12:9)

THE FATHER

I see where you are
Though you do not see,
Your face so downcast.
My face, you can't see.

Yet I am beside you,
Forever your friend.
My love does not change;
My love does not end.

I call you today.
I call … do you hear?
I speak to you now.
Do you realize I'm here?

Look to your Maker
Who's reaching to you
To carry your burdens
With a love that is true.

Let your heart be full
As you call on My name.
I'm still your Father
Whose love does not change.

LOOK UP

In the depth of sorrow,
There is this hope.
Though I feel forsaken,
I know this truth …
I am the apple of His eye,
The child who lost her way,
Yet even in my darkness,
Somehow, I learned to pray
A few words of hope.
I prayed He would hear
Even when I failed to see
He was always near.
My prayer reached heaven
As I began to see
Angels in all their glory
Looking down at me.
The Father never left you.
Though life has not been fair,
Look beyond this day.
Realize, He cares …
And as the tears fall,
As sometimes they do,
Look up to the heavens,
To your God, forever true.

NOT FORSAKEN

If I seem alone,
That may be true
But only in appearance.
I may seem forsaken
But not by God.
In Christ, I am surrounded
By a great cloud of witnesses
Cheering me on.
Even angels long to look
Into these things,
This glory of God ...
In earthen vessels,
Heaven rejoices over one sinner
Who comes to repentance.
So today, I am that sinner,
And Heaven is rejoicing
Because I was lost
But now am found
By an everlasting Father
Who will never leave me
Nor forsake me.

JESUS IS THE ANSWER

This is the day to move forward
Without looking back,
To fight for your future
Without regrets.
You've been through a lot,
But all things are working together
For your good in Christ.
So it is good to let go of the past,
Let go of your heartache,
Look to a brighter future.
Take God's hand,
And trust Him.
Even in our emptiness,
We find that God is
The Father to the fatherless,
The love that never fails.
So give it all to Him,
The good days and the bad,
For Jesus will always be …
The answer.

FATHER OF LIGHTS

Let the shadows fall,
One by one.
Let darkness fade
Into a new day
Let your light Oh God,
Shine in the dark places
Of my weary soul.
That I might understand
There are no shadows
In this light
Line upon line,
You speak life
Even as darkness
Tries to bring doubt,
I will hope in You.
Father of Lights,
The God of all
Of my yesterdays
Will keep me safe,
Today.

Every good gift and every perfect gift is from above, and comes down from the Father of lights, with whom there is no variation or shadow of turning. (James 1:17)

THE GRAVE

So also is the resurrection of the dead. The body is sown in corruption, it is raised in incorruption. It is sown in dishonor, it is raised in glory. It is sown in weakness, it is raised in power. It is sown in a natural body, it is raised a spiritual body.

—1 CORINTHIANS 15:47

othing rocks us to our core like death. It is the equalizer of humanity; we all must come to terms with it. No matter how great or successful you are, death has a way of humbling us and making us realize how little we control in this life. My first encounter with death would be the death of a child. Angela was born with spina bifida and had many medical issues, which would leave her with chest-down paralysis and many other complex medical problems as a result of it. But when she died in her sleep a few weeks before her eighth birthday, there would be no comfort in this world for my soul. I became familiar with the "valley of the shadow of death," and for a while, didn't know if I would ever come out of it. Death is never a visitor that you want to come, but it is one we all will face as we get older. When my daughter died in her sleep, I couldn't understand why then. I had carried her in the womb, knowing about her disabilities prior to her birth, secretly praying for God to cause me to miscarry, but that never happened. I was told she would be born with a very high lesion on her spine that would cause her to be paralyzed, and she already had a very severe curved spine and hydrocephalus (water on the brain). All of this was too much to think about, so I just prayed for God's will; surely, he didn't want me to have a child so malformed. But death would not come for her for many years. She lived for almost eight years, and during this time, I realized that not everyone had the same definition of "normal." My normal involved taking care of a very medically fragile child. But I learned to realize how wonderful it was to be *her* mom. She was special in every way and could light up a room. I've included some of my poetry about Angela in this section to memorialize her.

Years later, when my mother passed away, I again walked through a dark and lonely time. I have included poetry written after the deaths of my mother, my pastor, and my best friend. We all face death in some way or another; we learn to move on with our lives in the absence of that special person. The peace that God gives us in these circumstances is from knowing that death is not final; there is more.

This year I lost my pastor of many years; he died at forty-four years old. It was devastating to an entire church community in San Diego. I don't understand why this happened, but I know I will see him again. There is hope, even in death, because of the cross. The way has been made for us all to enter into the kingdom of heaven. So, although I grieve, I also rejoice to know that death is not the end. Yet death is still the unwanted visitor that comes to visit us and puts us in a state of grief, sometimes for years. Living in a world without that person is a painful existence; this is a testament to how much we have loved and lost.

I watched my mother-in-law grieve so deeply that I was not surprised when a few years later, she, too, passed away to be with her husband of over fifty years. We cannot measure grief by time; it is something that will always be in our lives if we loved someone that has passed from our life. Somehow, we learn to keep living in a world that seems empty without our loved one. When Angela died, I honestly couldn't imagine what life would be like. What I do remember was that I needed to grieve, and for me, that was just part of my life going forward. So, however you grieve, it is OK to not be OK. I know personally, the valley of the shadow of death can be hard to come out of.

This is my mother putting flowers on her
granddaughter Angela's grave.

THE GRAVE

In the quietness of earth, she lies
So still beneath my feet.
I say a silent prayer ...
Oh, grave, you bring such misery,
But here I am again
To mourn.

The grass is growing now.
The grave is not so new,
But I still remember
A better place and time
When she was more
Than just a memory
Marked by a stone.

Life goes on and on,
Yet time has stopped for me
As I sit here by a tree,
My life so intertwined
With this grave.

Yet death can never take
What she gave to me,
And I know that her life
Has forever changed mine,
And beyond this grave,
She lives.

ANGELA'S SONG

Though you're here but far away,
I know you'll make it through,
For the one who brought your soul this far
Is watching over you.
Though you may be small, too small to know
How much you are really loved,
We've prayed a prayer in Jesus's name
And trust in God above.
Angela, you're a special child,
And Jesus cares for you.
He brought you here to give Him glory
And prove that He is true,
That through His name, His precious name,
A miracle came true.
Angela, Oh Angela, that miracle is you.
Before you came into the world,
Your destiny was told
By men who could not see the Lord
Yet saw your little soul.
And now you're here by God's own hand
For He has seen you through,
And with each day that comes our way,
We know He's healing you.

LITTLE ANGEL

Why is she in a wheelchair?
Why is the sky so blue?
The Lord has all the answers.
I haven't got a clue.

Why is she always smiling?
I guess that you can say
She really must be happy
Just sitting there that way.

She is the consolation.
Her smile is our reward.
She is a ray of sunshine,
A blessing from the Lord.

Why is she in a wheelchair?
We don't always understand,
But she's our little angel
Designed by God's own hand.

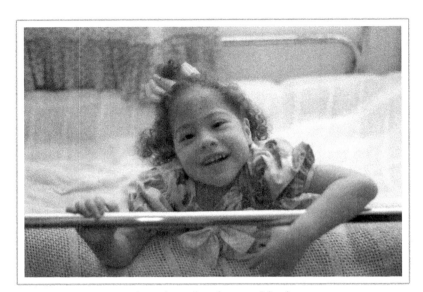

Angela in her hospital bed.

Angela in her wheelchair.

A BETTER PLACE IN TIME

The sky is not empty;
All is not lost.
By faith, we see the divine
When our heart is aching.
When we cannot see,
A path is revealed in time.
Hope is the cure to a sad disease
That tries to take our minds.
Though we struggle now,
The strength He gives
Will keep us in these times.
Take a step forward,
Believing in Him
Whose heart is ever kind.
God of tomorrows;
God of today.
Be the strength we find
When we cannot see,
Please lead the way
To a better place …
In time.

THE OPEN DOOR

Beyond all time and measure,
There is a place I know
Where heaven's gates are open
And blessings freely flow.

Beyond the cares of life,
There is a One so true
Who looks beyond your sadness
And sees the real you.

In your struggle, He is with you.
He knows that you are weak.
He's carried all of your burdens.
He understands your grief.

Beyond this tribulation,
There is an open door
Where we will live forever,
Rejoicing evermore.

OKAASAN

Mom

Okaasan
Sometimes …
I don't want
To turn the page
When I realize
You're no longer here.
Who am I now without you?
I miss your voice,
Your laughter, your stories
Forever etched in my heart,
And as life goes on,
Everything I am, or will be,
Is a homage to you.
Always here in my heart.
The way I live each day,
The heritage of my story,
The songs of my childhood,
The celebration of my culture,
These are the memories
Forever in my soul …
Okaasan.

FOREVER, YOUR FRIEND

I remember from years gone by,
The Sunday morning calls.
"Are you going to church today?"
Sometimes it was "yes," sometimes it was "no."
But most of the time, I just appreciated
That there was a person out there who cared.
Through her own struggles, she still thought of others.
Even when life had let her down,
Her faith in God was unwavering.
So today, my friend, I say, thank you
For sharing your passion for Him and reaching out to me,
Even when I was running away from God.
Thank you for the laughter.
For the times we laughed until we cried,
For bringing joy to us by just being who you are.
It is with heavy hearts that we release you today
To be with that one great love of your life … Jesus Christ.
I pray your legacy continues on in all of us you've touched,
Those of us who were able to witness your life as a ministry,
A ministry of caring for others and bringing laughter in hard times.
May you forever find comfort in the arms of God.
Until we meet again … forever, your friend.

Written in memory of my friend, Monica Torres
October 17, 1960 – February 10, 2015

BECAUSE HE LIVES

God heal the sadness
Weeping has endured.
Grief has overwhelmed us.
We give you the glory,
For in our weakness,
You are strong.
There is life beyond this grief;
There is hope beyond this pain.
Let us look forward
To a new beginning.
Let joy come as we realize
We are one day closer
To the kingdom of heaven.
Let Your kingdom come.
Lord, help us to cope
With sorrow and grief
As we move forward.
Let us never forget this truth—
God's children live on in eternity.
We have hope beyond this life
Because He lives.

GONE HOME

Some days, I struggle
With finding hope.
Where did it go?
Is there hope after loss?

Tomorrow, I will hope again,
But I just can't today.
Memories of what could be
Haunt me when I pray.

Lord, let me see more clearly,
Your hand is guiding me.
Today, I feel the struggle,
Please help my unbelief.

I miss those that have gone
Yet know they are with you
And wonder if it's wrong
To wish it were not true.

I miss those happy smiles.
The faithful and the few
Important in my life
Gone home to be with You.

THE SHEPHERD

So many times …
We forget how fortunate we are
To have a pastor who watches over us.
We forget to say thank you
For visiting me in the hospital,
Thank you for texting me
To see how I was doing,
Thank you for being my friend,
For not judging me
When I became distracted by life.
You reached out to me,
You made me realize that
God still cares about me,
Even when I fall short
Of the calling of God in my life.
You remind me …
Is there a poem from the Lord?
As David said, "Is there not a cause?"
We were blessed that
You reminded us of this.
You were a great pastor …
A leader and a friend
Who reached out to everyone
In every station of life.
You were authentic and true,
The man God called you to be.
Southeast San Diego's own.
A great man of God
who fulfilled his calling,
You fought for souls with every breath
Every day of the week,
Never ceasing to minister
To the needs of the lost

Stirring our hearts
For the cause of Christ.
We can't imagine
Going forward without you,
But we will
Because this is who we are.
The sinners who became saints
Under the watchful eye …
Of a shepherd.

Written in memory of Pastor Shaunte Cephus.
August 29, 1978–October 2, 2022

IV

THE ABYSS

*Why are you cast down, O my soul? And why are
you disquieted within me? Hope in God, for I shall
yet praise Him for the help of His countenance.*

—PSALMS 42:5

When I was seventeen, a kind woman brought me to an old-fashioned Pentecostal church. We later became friends, and in our conversations, she mentioned that she could see that I was depressed. This upset me to know that not only was I depressed, but others, too, could see it. I didn't know how to deal with my sadness as a teenager, so I escaped it with the help of my friends. But as an adult, I had to deal with it without escaping to go party with friends. I realized that my days of running were over, and I would need to deal with life. Prayer helped me not only realize that I could face the darkness but that God would help me through these dark times if I let him in. Later I would seek counseling and go on antidepressants, and it did help. But as time went on, there would be more losses, and I would struggle with the pain of losing a child, losing my mother, and later my best friend. We all have to navigate these waters of grief at some point in our lives.

Recently, I have had close friends and even family members who have committed suicide. There is no getting over these losses; we constantly look back and wish we could have done more to prevent these tragic events. Never allow thoughts of suicide to make you believe that no one loves you. There are always people who love you, and if you can't think of anyone, God loves you more than my words express. Take a step forward out of that mindset, and you'll see there are many reasons to believe God gave you for a purpose. Your darkness can help someone else realize that we all face depression sometimes.

There were times when I felt healing come through prayer. Realizing there is a God who loves you helps in those dark times. There have been times that I needed more, and medication did help as well. I believe in a multi-faceted approach in my life, but I still have bad days. Prayer has helped me to cope, and knowing God has made a huge difference in my life. So it is with these words that I will begin to allow others to look into some of these dark days when poetry allowed me to express myself. I don't stay in that mindset for too long; depression can be a rabbit hole that is hard to get out of. I have found solace in the scriptures, especially in the book of Psalms. David, in Psalms 42, encourages himself in the Lord, "Why are you cast down, O my soul?" Sometimes we need to dig ourselves out of the rabbit hole and realize that outside, the sun is shining. When you get out of the negative mindset of unbelief, you realize there are so many reasons to be thankful.

I try to start every day with prayer and have found that if I focus on God first, everything else seems to fall into place. Some of us may have a predisposition toward depression for various reasons. I am no professional, so I can only speak from personal experience. I have fought these issues all of my life and can say that I have made peace with them. I try to stay away from the edge, so to speak. I don't look too hard into the darkness and ask why anymore. God knows why; we just need to focus on Him and allow Him to lead us away from the dark thoughts of depression.

THE ABYSS

There is a place I know too well,
A place of emptiness,
Of shattered dreams and broken lives,
A place called the abyss.

So many people live there,
And it's deep within their soul.
They live a life of emptiness
And never become whole.

No one wants to be there,
But somehow, they are snared
And believe there is no hope in life
And no one really cares.

And I've heard an old saying
That I've found to be true,
That when you look into the abyss,
It looks back into you.

But there is someone who cares,
Who calls us from afar.
He stands with open arms;
He loves us as we are.

So you don't have to live
In a place so void of love,
God robed himself in flesh
And descended from above.

He paid the price for you,
To set you free from sin.
His love is everlasting;
He loves your soul within.

The abyss is always there.
If you look hard, you will see.
We all have been there once or twice,
But some will never leave.

From the end of the earth will I cry unto You, When my heart is overwhelmed; Lead me to the rock that is higher than I. (Psalms 61:2)

THE LIE

If evil were a place
It would be somewhere dark,
Hiding from the light,
Whispering lies.

Corroding our thoughts,
Killing our dreams,
Crushing our hopes
With fear.

An endless abyss,
A place of despair
Where we believe
A lie.

Let the light in.
Let this be the day
You overcome
The pain.

If evil were a place
It would be somewhere dark.
Step into the light.
Don't believe the lie.

WORD OF HOPE

The darkness in my life, the sorrow of my soul,
The never-ending sadness that I cannot control.
I search my heart for hope; where is the light of day?
I know God has the answer, so I begin to pray.

Is there a meaning in this madness?
Is there healing for my soul?
Can you take away this sadness?
Will I ever be made whole?

I hear the Spirit whisper in my presence, there is joy.
My love can heal your sorrow; my love can fill this void.
Look up to the heavens … it is not an empty sky.
There's a God who hears your prayer
And hears you when you cry.

Surely, I have walked with you
Through valleys, through the night
When darkness tries to steal your joy.
Remember, I'm the light.

You are a child of God, and you belong to Me.
Perfect love casts out all fear, and truth will set you free.
The awesome Word of God, the truth that lights the way.
Thank You, Lord, for answering every time I pray.

THE BATTLE

You are a God
Who answers prayer.
Even in the silence,
There is an answer.
I will wait on you
For direction,
And I give to you
All of my broken dreams
For therein lies the secret
To my peace.
Dark thoughts
Try to overtake me,
But then I remember …
There is hope beyond this life
Because Jesus paid the price.
There will be an eternity,
And there we will know
Eternal life without pain.
The answer was always
To give everything—
The good, the bad,
And the broken—
To Him.

GRAY DAYS

Emptiness and sorrow
Just seem to find a way
To enter in the picture.
Life has turned to gray.

Where is the God who saved me?
I hear a voice within.
My pain is overwhelming.
My unbelief, a sin.

Help me, Lord, to realize
Your grace will see me through.
Beyond this present darkness,
There is still a sky that's blue.

Within this bitter sadness,
You are the sweet reward.
The hope of new beginnings
Is knowing You, oh Lord.

WALKING IN THE LIGHT

. . . .

I pray …
Let there be
Goodness in my life
That overtakes the darkness
In my mind.
Let my thoughts
Be free of fear.
Let there be hope
That I will see
The goodness of God
In the land of the living.
Let there be light
In a dark place,
Even if it is my mind.
Let me realize
There are no shadows
When I walk in the light.

A NEW DAY

Let the dawn of a new day
Remind us that yesterday is gone,
And with each new day,
There is an opportunity to know You.
By Your stripes, we are healed.

Lord, heal our broken hearts today,
Wash away our sorrows,
Let us lift up our heads to
Look into heaven and believe
You have forgiven our sins
And removed their effects.

Let our minds be healed
From the sins of yesterday.
Let us walk in the light
Of this glorious new day.
Let us come to a realization,
The past is gone under the blood.
There are no more shadows.
We have a new life in Christ,
And His mercies are new each day.

THE WORD OF LIFE

Lord, help me to face the darkness,
The shadow of despair
That has followed me through time.
Help me to realize that faith
Is the substance of things hoped for.
Faith can chase away every shadow.
It has been many years
This darkness has followed me.
Where is the hope of yesterday?
Did I bury it in the ground
With my loved ones?
But I hear your Spirit calling,
"Do not let the enemy steal the seed of faith
Buried deep within your heart, it is but
A mustard seed, yet within it
There is hope for tomorrow."
Though darkness is great all around me,
Within I have the seed of life.
The powerful Word of God says,
"All things are possible," and "I can do all
Things through Christ who strengthens me."
"If God is for us, who can be against us?"
Lord, let that seed continue to grow.
Let Your Word prevail in my life
Till the shadows pass.

DELIVERANCE

Hear my cry, oh God,
For I am in a dark place.
I need your love today.
Let me realize, above all,
My hope is in You.
You have answered,
Though I could not see it.
My heart was crushed,
But You led me out
Of my dark despair.
You have been my shelter
And have surrounded me
With songs of deliverance.
You hold me in Your arms
And carry me through
The dark valley of loss.
You keep me in a secret place
Where I find rest
Under Your shadow.
So let the storm rage on
For You will ever keep me
With a love divine.
You are the living God
Who delivers my soul
From darkness.

V

TRUTH

If you abide in my word, you are my disciples indeed. And you shall know the truth, and the truth shall make you free.

—JOHN 8:31

When I look back at what started me on the journey to know God, one of the most important aspects of my beginning was a hunger to know the truth. Where it all began was with a hunger to know the truth about God; if He was real, I was going to find out. Coupled with that hunger, there also needs to be a little bit of faith. His Word still communicates His will to us, His redemptive plan, and His faithfulness; it is all there in the scripture. More than just words on a page, God breathes life into His Word and speaks to us today through the Bible.

Much of my poetry is based on the Word of God, especially in this chapter. Principles that spoke to me in scripture made their way to the page. Some poetry is directed to the body of Christ, which is the church. It may not be easily understood by the "unchurched," nor is it meant to bring condemnation to anyone. I believe God gave me these poems for a reason, and many have been shared with churches.

I have tried to respect all religious beliefs because, as I mentioned earlier, I was raised a Buddhist. There are so many beliefs in the world. But after spending my entire life not knowing who Jesus Christ is, I began to desire to know if there was a God outside of what little I knew about Him. I had the desire to know what the truth was, even if it wasn't what I wanted to hear. It was a slow process of many little prayers prayed in my mind. *God, if you're real, reveal yourself to me.* He did do that for me in time; it wasn't overnight but a process of many years of spending time with God in prayer. If you are searching for truth, I recommend prayer. Even if you don't initially feel anything, in time, you will see the difference those prayers have made in your life.

Jesus said, "If you abide in my word, you are my disciples indeed." This might be hard to do at first, but it is important that you learn how to "abide" in His Word to know the truth. So much has been said to discredit the Bible and Christianity that you won't know where to start. I started by reading the Gospel of John, and it gave me insight into how crucial the Word of God is, as it starts with, "In the beginning was the Word, and the Word was with God, and the Word was God" (John 1:1). Just as when you write what is on your heart down on paper, God's Word represents the heart of God. You cannot separate my thoughts from me, nor can you separate God's thoughts from Him. I say all this for those free-spirited souls who have a difficult time believing God's Word to be true. In the book of Isaiah, God speaks through the prophet and declares, "For My thoughts are not your thoughts, nor are your ways My ways, says the Lord." We have so much to gain by learning about the truths in the Bible, and by following the pattern given in John 8:31, "You shall know the truth, and the truth shall make you free."

I have found that those who desire truth will eventually find it, and having a hunger for truth is a good thing. Sometimes we can muddy the waters with too many man-made additions to what we think of as truth. The Bible is the last word when it comes to what the Lord expects of us, and how we can know Him in a more personal way. If you just open your Bible and read it for yourself, you will have taken the first step in knowing what truth is.

MOTHER OF ZION

Arms of love
That can heal all pain.
How I love you,
Mother of Zion,
Called by His name.
In my search, I found
Your warm embrace.
You simply loved
Beyond color or race.
You taught me how
To call on His name,
And in that moment,
How all things changed.
I love to hear you pray.
Hear you say,
"Child, God will take
Care of everything."
And the angels sing
As you pray.
My church, my home
Is in your loving embrace.

SOMEONE WHO REALLY CARES

I am your Sunday visitor
Who comes through your church door.
I have no fame or fortune,
In fact, I may be poor.

But in my soul, I'm searching
For something I can't find.
To make my peace with God;
To have some peace of mind.

My prayer is just to be a part
Of your church family,
But I don't know where to start.
I'm from the "world," you see.

Please don't forget to greet me
For I, too, am very shy.
In fact, I may sneak out the door
Before you even try.

So next time that you see me,
Please say a silent prayer.
And remember, I am searching
For someone who really cares.

CAST THE FIRST STONE

How is it that we
Have become so cold?
Have we separated ourselves
From the world
To the point that we cannot
Cross the divide to reach a soul?
How is it that we
Call ourselves Christians
When in actuality
There is a lack
Of the very essence
Of who Christ is?
Jesus said,
"You who are without sin
Cast the first stone."
You may think that you
Have the right
To cast that stone
Of judgment,
But in actuality, you do not.
Your sin is, in fact,
That you lack this truth …
God is love.

THE SHORTNESS OF TIME

The hands of time are reaching,
And they reach to a world that is lost
From the beginning of time, we know
From a Savior who died on a cross.

The hands of time are pointing
To the dawn of a brand new day,
When all things will become new
And old things will all pass away.

But who in that day will be ready
When Jesus will beckon us home?
Will we hear the sound of that trumpet?
Or will our hearts be cold as a stone?

I hear the voice of the Savior,
And He's calling to your heart and mine.
Are you sure that your soul will be ready?
Do you realize the shortness of time?

WHERE IS THE LIGHT?

Look beyond yourself today,
Beyond your religion.
Don't let tradition overtake you.
There is a world
Who doesn't care
How holy you are,
But they are searching …
Where is the light?

Where is Christ
In your religious activities?
The world is dark
And growing darker every day.
Yes, you can speak in tongues,
But where is the light?

Pierce the darkness
With God's love.
Show kindness to a "sinner."
Reach beyond your comfort zone.
Only the pure love of God
Can pierce this night,
So as you curse the darkness,
Let me ask you …
Where is the light?

HOLINESS

Holiness is not a form
Or fashion you can wear.
It's not just how you dress
Or if you cut your hair.

But from within the heart,
God's Spirit teaches all
To guide us with a loving hand,
To keep us if we fall.

So it is we truly see
God cleanses us from sin
And gives to us a brand-new life
With a heart that pleases Him.

ONE BODY

What is this?
Religious subculture?
But a line that divides,
Simply put …
People
Who can't reach
Outside of their own
Comfort zone
Are wrong.
Anything
That divides a body
Of believers
Should be checked
At the door.
Leave your opinions,
Your prejudices
At home
When you come
To God's house.
Or better yet,
Leave that mindset
Altogether.

THE CALL

To everything, there is a time.
The Word of God proclaims
It is our time to manifest
The power of His name.

The time has come to rise.
I hear the Father say,
"Manifest My love;
Teach the world to pray."

Is there no balm in Gilead
To heal the hurting soul?
"Manifest My power,
And let Me take control."

The hurting and the lost
Are passing every day.
Will you be my hands?
Will you stop and pray?

THE HOPE OF GLORY

God is greater than
Religion or traditions of men,
He is greater than
Religious subcultures.
Hope has been lost,
In a dark sea of unbelief.
What the world needs to see,
Is Christ in you,
The hope of glory
Not tradition, but truth
A living God, breathing
On the inside of you.
Show forth His fruit.
Manifest His Power.
And the pure love of God
Will bring an anointing
Of love and grace
To set us free
From the bondage
Of religion

SHADES OF GRAY

Sometimes we walk in darkness
When we are in the light.
Sometimes we fail to see
There is no wrong or right.
Sometimes the path's not clear,
We cannot see the way.
Sometimes life isn't black or white
But many shades of gray.
But Lord, I want to know You.
I want to do Your will.
I know that I have failed,
But help me serve You still.
Life's not always easy,
But help me to obey.
Let me do Your will
Through many shades of gray.

VI

WORSHIP

You worship what you do not know; we know what we worship, for salvation is of the Jews. But the hour is coming, and now is, when the true worshippers will worship the Father in spirit and truth; for the Father is seeking such to worship Him. God is a Spirit, and those who worship Him must worship in spirit and in truth.

—JOHN 4:22–24

Although I knew little about my mother's Buddhism and the philosophical reasons behind it, I bowed down before a butsudan in worship, as did all my sisters. I remember when I was very young, walking with my neighbor friend to the nearby thrift shop. Looking in the window, there was a picture of Jesus on the cross. I asked her, "Who is that?"

She asked, "You have never heard of Jesus?"

I said, "No."

She began to grill me about church and religious beliefs like I was a heathen. My father was not a religious man, and though he disagreed with Buddhism, he didn't want to anger my mother. So that day I learned about how Jesus died on a cross from a picture at goodwill, but I still didn't understand why.

Religion can be a ritual when we become so familiar with traditions that they become ceremonial. This type of religion satisfies our need to be religious but our hearts may not be in it. True worship is done from the heart. We give God praise as we worship and thank Him for all that He has done. Worship is what brings the presence of God into the room. This can be done in corporate worship or in your own prayer closet. Worshipping God in spirit and in truth involves our hearts.

Another aspect of worship and praise involves music. I believe some powerful lyrics lead us into the presence of God. I sometimes play worship music during my prayer time. When you give God praise in your prayer time, it changes you, and that evolution will change you into a worshipper. When God is at the center of your life, and you lift him up in praise, not everyone will understand; that is why it is important to go to a church that believes in corporate worship. But you can praise him anywhere, with or without music, even at home during your prayer time. To worship God is to be the recipient of all God is. I have been healed of serious debilitating illnesses while worshipping God. We gain everything in exchange when we give him praise.

One of the greatest kings in the Bible, David, was a worshipper. He wrote many of the psalms and incorporated music into the worship of the temple. Many of the psalms in the Bible were sung as worship songs. There was such deep praise from David that God called him a man after his own heart. David had his failures but knew how to pray and repent; he also knew there was a secret place of the highest found through worship.

I have realized in some of the darkest times in my life that worship within my private prayer time would become a way for me to find peace and rest. I had trouble worshipping in public in the Pentecostal church I went to in the beginning, but found that when I learned to worship in my private prayer time, that would help me not only overcome my pride but would usher me into the presence of God in a way that I didn't think possible. Many of my fears and insecurities were unable to remain in the presence of God. King David, in the book of Psalms, said, "You will show me the path of life; In Your presence is fullness of joy; At your right hand are pleasures forevermore" (Psalms 16:11). There is nothing greater than worshipping a living God who visits you in your prayer time.

TRUE WORSHIP

Speak to the Lord.
Reach out to Him today.
Thirst for Him.
Even if you are empty,
Pour out your soul,
And the miracle of God's fire
Will be poured out on you.
When the Spirit troubles
The waters in your soul,
That is the moment
Of your miracle.
Don't miss the moment.
Offer up to God
All that you are.
Let the fire of His Spirit
Be poured out on you today,
And as you offer to Him
All that you are,
Be filled with all
That He is.

THE OFFERING

Lord, I lift You up.
Let Your name forever be praised.
Your love ever be the lens
I view my life through.
It's not about me; it's about the lost.
About the cross
And love that continues to reach
Throughout time.

The great God of heaven
Who came to dwell among us,
And for a time … we beheld His glory.
How could we know the plan?
The God of creation laying down
His life for us?
Everything in man
Would try to stop it.

Yet the plan remained;
His love unchanged.
And throughout ages of time,
His love still speaks
From an old rugged cross.
Our God, who became
The offering.

IN HIS IMAGE

Lord, I give You the glory
As I worship today,
Remembering the cross
And what it represents—
A loving Savior,
Reaching out to mankind.
Ministry that goes beyond the grave;
Ministry that lives on in eternity.
To lift You up to others,
To do the work of God
From a pure heart.
Break the chains of religion,
The chains that keep us bound
To a form of godliness
Without power.
Let us rise from the ashes
Of religion
Into Your image.

THANKFUL

To everything that
Brought me to this place,
I am thankful
For the pain, the heartache
That made me
Reach out to You …
God, I am thankful
That I survived
The tests and trials
Living in this world.
Thank You for Your protection,
For angels in my life.
Thank You that I have breath
To give You praise today.
I pray for Your blessings
On souls great and small,
That You would mend
The broken heart,
Lift the broken spirit.
Heal us, Lord,
Open our eyes to see
It is by Your grace
That we are here today
To be thankful.

ANOINT ME

Anoint me for change … for the place I need to be.
Let it flow within my life; let it set the captive free.
Let it bring the hope that all the years
Of my life were not in vain.
I am standing on the edge of things to come.
Thy will be done …

Anoint me to share Your holy word with all.
It is a sin to hold within the greatness of Your call.
Your Word can heal the coldest soul.
Your Word has changed my life.
In darkness now, I share Your Word of light.
Help me fight …

Anoint me to share Your everlasting love,
To reach a soul who's lost. Lord, bless me from above.
There is a world so dark in sin that hope cannot be found.
Anoint my words to share Your love today.
For this, I pray …

VII

FORGIVENESS

For if you forgive men their trespasses, your heavenly Father will also forgive you. But if you do not forgive men their trespasses, neither will your Father in heaven forgive your trespasses.

—MATTHEW 6:14–15

Unforgiveness is like cancer in our hearts. As a teenager, I was angry at the world. This would lead me to do a lot of things that I would later regret. It would take many years for me to realize I was really angry. I was going through a rebellious stage that would do a lot of damage to my life. At the core of this anger was resentment toward my father for leaving our family. In actuality, my parents had grown apart from so many military deployments. My mother, by this time, was a very active member of her Buddhist community, and my father was a severe alcoholic. But I was only ten when my parents split up, so I didn't understand. I remember my mother praying in front of her butsudan, crying uncontrollably, and it broke me; these wounds would not heal easily.

Forgiveness is intentional; we can't bury our resentments and hatred and expect them to disappear. Unforgiveness can become hatred, which changes us, and we become hard-hearted. Hate unchecked can manifest itself in many ways. Bigotry is a form of hatred I have never understood. How people can judge another race incompetent is wrong. The enemy of our souls rejoices when he can plant these seeds of hatred in individuals that last for generations. This is a form of hatred that is ignorant. To counter such ignorance with more hatred is not healthy for us; God will judge those who hate.

I have had difficulty forgiving those who have wronged me. But I have found unforgiveness to be a weight on my soul. We carry these wrongs in our hearts to our own detriment; the only way to be free of those who have hurt us is to forgive. Realize that people will fail (some even with bigoted hearts full of hate); only God is perfect. When we forgive, we are living our lives as Christ did, who forgave from the cross as he was crucified. The Bible says, "Love will cover a multitude of sins" (1 Peter 4:8). As God covered our sins with the blood of Christ, so should we cover our enemies with forgiveness.

Having said all this, I realize that there are some things that God will have to help us to forgive others for. It is easier said than done. What I've found when I'm having trouble forgiving and getting past an offense is that it helped me to forgive if I prayed for them. What was even more surprising was that God would begin to move in the person's life, and I could see a change. This would help me to realize that God can change people, and people are not all inherently evil; there is hope for humanity. There will still be some people who will never change and become angry that you aren't participating in their hatred. God knows how to deal with people, just pray for God to bless them anyway. It will help you to heal and become better for it. We can't win everyone, and not everyone is going to like us, so we have to realize this and move on with our lives. Haters are going to hate, so there's that.

A PRAYER OF FORGIVENESS

Lord, let me forgive
As You forgave,
Not with an agenda in mind
But in the purest form of letting go
Of all wrongs … even those hurts
Which have yet to heal.
I speak forgiveness and healing
To my own soul.
To those who have let me down,
I am sorry that I expected so much.
Only God can be all things
To all people.
I release you to be who you are,
And I pray for your healing, as well,
In a world of broken promises.
You, Lord are the only One
Who remains forever true.
I choose to forgive
As You have forgiven me.

WOUNDS

Sometimes …
The depth of sorrow,
The root of bitterness
Comes from a place
That is broken,
A place of emptiness
And disappointments.
As time passes, we understand
We can only love
If we have known love.
The heart cannot give
What it does not have.
A generation passes.
What is left behind?
With clarity and compassion,
Forgive the failures of others.
Emptiness is a state of mind.
Love is a choice.
Heal a wounded spirit.
Heal a broken heart.
Heal yourself … and forgive.

CONTRAST

What are we
But pieces of each other?
Fibers in the greater cause
That is this life.
What am I without you?
For your differences
Make me complete.
I ask you not to change
Who you are
But to understand
These contrasts in life
Make us who we are.
We all are given free will,
Which is given to us
By a merciful Creator.
So I honor your decision.
As I pray, you honor mine.
Blessed is the peacemaker
Who strives to understand
It's not about being right ...
It's about being more
Like Him.

FORGIVENESS

Why is it so hard to say
I'm sorry?
Is it our pride
That keeps us apart?
Has unforgiveness
Become a way of life?
Love can cover
A multitude of sins,
But unforgiveness hurts
As it looks for more reasons
To hold onto pain.
What bitterness
We bring our souls
In the name of revenge.
I pray that I can be
Soft enough to feel pain
But mature enough
To forgive.
Heal my heart, Lord,
With a little love
And forgiveness

THE PROCESS

Would to God …
That I could go back in time,
Would It be the same?
Would I change my mind?
Would to God …
That I held my tongue
Before speaking from my heart
When my heart was hurting
From wounds unspoken.
I try to forget …
But it's still there
Under the surface,
Waiting to arise
From the depths of my soul.
I need time to heal,
Time to accept and realize
That life is not over.
Though I fall,
I shall yet arise
And walk in the light
Of His love.

FATHER FORGIVE US

Father, forgive them
For not knowing that You are real.
We see through a glass darkly,
But they don't see at all.
Open their eyes to see You,
Not just in Your creation,
But in the beauty of a God
Who forgives from a cross.
Father, forgive us
For not understanding Your love,
The intricacy of Your plan,
So divine we cannot fathom it.
Forgive us for our unbelief
For You have fulfilled
The law and the prophets
With a sacrificial lamb.
You have given us
The hope of forgiveness.
Help us to open our eyes
To the truth that is before us,
The One who lived and died,
Not just to mark the times
But to open heaven's gates
To mankind for eternity.

LOAVES AND FISHES

There is a lad here who has five barley loaves and two small fish, but what are they among so many?

—JOHN 6:9

The young boy in this story gave his lunch to Jesus and watched Him feed five thousand people from his five loaves and a few small fish. I have gathered about forty years of poetry while putting this book together. I pray that my poems help someone realize God is still speaking today and wants to bless whatever life we have to give Him. I pray this book conveys a positive message to counter all the negativity we deal with on a daily basis. God wants to give you hope and speak life to you. We all need to hear this message of hope and realize that God loves us. I wrote a song many years ago about this Bible story. Like the boy in this story, if all I have to give is a word of encouragement through poetry, I pray that God will breathe on this meager offering and let it speak to every heart that reads this book. My loaves and fish all these years, whatever talent God allotted me, seemed to come through writing songs and poetry. I have included some of these songs in this section of the book.

I have studied the world's great literature over the past few years, yet nothing compares to the Bible. It has been a great source of inspiration for me. Scripture is timeless and speaks in an elevated tone to the masses as well as the individual. It is exciting when God speaks directly to you through His Word. The Bible has an entire book of poetry in Psalms, which offers a glimpse of how a great Hebrew king encouraged us to praise God in our dark times. Beyond this, there is also a treasure of literature that speaks to us through the wisdom of great men inspired by God. These words inspired much of my poetry, and God, in prayer throughout my life, has led me in this direction of self-expression through poetry. We are made in His image and likeness, so I have to believe that God is a poet.

Thank you for going on this journey with me and reading my book. It wasn't easy to write, but I pray it will be easier to read. Like David, I have laid out my life in the words on the page; the good, the bad, and the darkest days. Those poems that I wrote in secret, I pray, will reach all of those they were intended for. May God take these poems and make a difference in someone's life today; they are my "Loaves and Fishes."

With that said, I hope and pray that I inspire you to do whatever God has called *you* to do. Whether it is just that first step toward Christ or something you have been feeling God speak to you about. We all start somewhere on this journey, and my purpose in writing has to be greater than just poetic expression but to change a life. So if I change one life through writing that is enough for me. What I find fascinating is that God has been speaking to us all throughout our lives, yet sometimes we don't realize it was the voice of God leading us in a certain direction. I believe we all have the capacity to hear the voice of God if we focus our minds and heart on Him. Whatever that something is for you that you feel that you can contribute to the cause of Christ, let God use you in your gifts. You might just be the one that feeds the multitude.

LOAVES AND FISHES

Once there was a little lad who came to hear the Master's words.
He brought with him his tiny lunch of fish and barley loaves.
He gave it all to Jesus, and Jesus broke the bread.
On that day, the Master blessed, and everyone was fed.

(Chorus)
Lord, please take my loaves and fishes and take everything I am.
Make me a new creature created by Your hands.
And Lord, if I've given everything, I pray that You will bless.
Take my meager offering and give it to the rest.

No longer do I see myself with all my many needs
When, Lord, there are so many more out there for You to feed.
So please, take whatever I can give, and I pray that You will bless.
Take my meager offering and give it to the rest.

(Bridge)
And though I may not have too much,
I pray that You will add Your touch.
Let everything I give to You
Turn into so much more.

THE STAGE

The world is a stage,
So play your part,
And choose your destiny.
If we all are merely players,
What will your part be?

Will you play the role of Christ
As you press on toward your goals?
While you're reaching for that star,
Are you reaching out to souls?

Remember godly teachings
You learned on chapel days.
Remember all the good times;
Remember how to pray.

Play your part and play it well,
But heed the Spirit's call,
And let the Lord be center stage
Before the curtain falls.

EVERYTHING YOU'LL EVER NEED

Time can heal all wounds, I've heard so many say.
Yet there are some things in our hearts that time can't take away.
Jesus knows your heartaches, even those you try to hide,
For His love has stood the test of time.

(Chorus 1)
Open up your heart to the one who can take away
Every sorrow you have known. When you thought you were alone,
He was there, right there to give you everything.
Everything you'll ever need is in the Lord.

So, if your heart is broken and your dreams have not come true,
Give your life back to the One who gave His life for you.
There's no other love like Jesus; He's the one you're waiting for.
He is everything you'll ever need, everything and more.

(Chorus 2)
Open up your heart to the one who can take away
Every sorrow you have known. When you thought you were alone,
He was there, right there to give you everything.
Everything you'll ever need is in the Lord.
Yes, He'll be there, right there to give you everything …
Everything you'll ever need is in the Lord.

MY OWN IDENTITY

I may not be like you,
But I'm a lot like me.
I am quite unique,
With my own identity.

I may not be perfect,
But Jesus loves me still.
And each day, I try to live
According to His will.

So, if I seem different,
That, my friend, may be.
Remember, I'm a person
With my own identity.

WHERE EAGLES FLY

A dreamer, yes to many, I've dreamed of bluer skies.
But now, I finally see myself, now I realize,
Without You, I am nothing, like a bird with broken wings.
I pray, Oh Lord, You'll help me now to give You everything.

(Chorus 1)
Lord, I want to soar again with You to the place I used to know,
Where the cares of this life fade away, and I learned how to let go.
I want to soar above the clouds to a higher place in You,
Where it won't matter anymore what people say or do.
I'm in the sky where eagles fly.

The days are growing shorter; we're running out of time.
Too many now are on the ground, having forgotten how to fly.
They look up to the heavens and remember better days
As they soar into a secret place and give You all the praise.

(Chorus 2)
Lord, I want to soar where eagles fly, but must I fly alone?
So many just don't understand it's time now to go home.
Soon we'll soar above the clouds to a higher place in You,
Where it won't matter anymore what people say or do.
I'm in the sky, where eagles fly.

AN ANGEL FOR ME

Tiny fingers, tiny toes,
Little eyes, and a little nose.
Who can she be?
She looks a lot like me.
I know that she belongs to You,
But in my heart, I know it's true,
She's Your gift to me …
Thank You, Lord.

(Chorus)
Heaven is blessing on earth here below.
A sweet little angel that we can watch grow.
Ribbons and lace curls around her face.
Life's greatest blessings are free.
A sweet little angel for me.

So today, we celebrate
In our hearts, we dedicate
This little one within our hands.
We give to You, Lord,
God of all forever true,
We dedicate her life to You,
This little angel we so adore.
Thank You, Lord.

CHANGED

God, You are the same
Yesterday, today, and forever.
Your love never changes,
Even as You stand with open arms
To a world that can't comprehend
Your great love.
Forever it remains,
Regardless of who we are
Or what we've done.
That love that led You to the cross
Never changes
As we grow and change.
I pray we take a closer look
At the cross,
What it represents,
More than a token of Your love,
But redemption for all
Great and small.
Can come and kneel at the cross
And forever be …
Changed.

SEIZE THE DAY

A new day dawns.
Yesterday is diminishing.
Is it such a tragedy,
To leave it behind.
Yesterday forever gone.
Thank God,
Sufficient thereunto
Was the evil thereof.
What will you do with this day?
For it too shall pass
And be a memory before long.
Seize the day.
Look around you;
Life is beautiful.
We are wonderfully made.
Each cell, every molecule of life
Contain the secrets of eternity.
Yesterday brought tragedy and loss …
But a new day is dawning,
And as for me,
I will rejoice.

IX

THE LOVE OF GOD

Behold what manner of love the Father has bestowed on us that we should be called the children of God! Therefore the world does not know us, because it did not know Him.

—1 JOHN 3:1

I have struggled with my identity all my life. It might have something to do with being raised by a single parent marginalized by American culture. It might be because I had to sometimes serve as an interpreter for my mother, *even* when she was speaking English. Or it might be because, growing up as a child of an alcoholic father, I felt invisible; I am not sure why. But when I came upon the scripture above in the first book of John, I realized that my identity was now so much more than who my natural parents were. No matter how many mistakes I made as a teenager, I had still become a child of God. The blood of Christ was greater than all of my mistakes.

God's love would begin reaching out to me through dreams, and even through the poetry that I had written as a teenager. It wasn't until many years later that I would actually understand God's love in my life. At twenty-two years old, one year after getting married, I would find out that the child I was carrying was severely handicapped. I automatically blamed myself, and even some of my friends in the church asked if I thought it was from all the drugs I took as a teenager. I felt cursed during my pregnancy and prayed for a miscarriage. I remember wishing I would go to sleep and never wake up the next day, but thankfully, I did.

Years later, I can see how that little girl not only changed my life but caused my mom to ask me about heaven. My mother, a devout Buddhist, wanted to see her granddaughter Angela again. I believe it even made her hope that there was a heaven. In my mother's last days on earth, when I would say prayers for her, she would bow her head, which still amazes me to this day. There might be surprises in heaven, and I believe she will get that opportunity to see her granddaughter Angela again.

The love of God is greater than any darkness that tries to destroy us. It is only by the grace of God that I did not become a drug addict like many of my closest friends. But even if I had, I believe God's love is greater than addiction. Where ever we fall short, God's grace is abundant, and He knows what is in our hearts. If you truly want to be free from addiction, God can break addiction off of your life.

John also said that because the world did not know Christ or recognize Him as the Savior, it would not know us. Living for God in a lost world can get lonely. But the Bible says, "He who is in you is greater than he who is in the world" (1 John 4:4). Recognizing the spiritual realm is half of the battle. Nothing is ever easy; that is why faith is so important. The love of God is tangible and felt in His presence when we sincerely pray. Worship is a door that can open up spiritual blessings to you. Once you realize that God is real and how much He loves you, prayer is not a chore but an opportunity to talk to your heavenly father who loves you.

THE LOVE OF GOD

We have heard Him speak,
Seen Him manifest in signs and wonders,
Yet even as we gaze into His glory,
Do we really know
The love of God?

We have felt His presence …
Even held it in our hands.
We have stood in awe of His glory,
Yet even as we give Him praise,
Do we really know
The love of God?

Ever reaching …
Everlasting …
The love of God
Reaches through time
To every heart and every soul
So that we, too, could know
There is hope in this life
Because of …
The love of God.

JESUS LOVES ME

He painted the world into existence,
He created the earth and the sky,
But my mind still can't help but wonder
The reason He loves you and I.

He hears the cry of the humble,
He listens to our every prayer,
Still, my heart just cannot fathom
Why the God of the universe cares.

I look to the cross, and I wonder.
There is so much I don't understand,
But in His great love, he has saved me
By His blood, my redemption was planned.

I look up into the heavens
And marvel at all that I see,
But greater still is just knowing
How much Jesus loves me.

GOD'S LOVE

God's love is …
Manifested in the simple things
A caring smile, a friendly face,
A soft answer.

God's love is …
Realizing it's not about you
But someone else
Who needs forgiveness,
Even as they manifest
Hatred and malice.

God's love is …
Expressed in more
Than the cross you wear;
It's the silent prayer as you crucify your flesh
So others might see Him.

God's love is …
From an everlasting Father,
Forever and true,
But will it manifest today
In you?

NEVER ALONE

Alone again,
I find myself wondering,
Is this the way
It was meant to be?
Alone again,
I find myself wondering
Why?
But loneliness
Only brings me closer
To a realization
Of who You are to me.
When everyone
Walks out the door,
You are still here.
Alone again,
I find a place to pray,
And it is there
I realize …
I'm never alone.

THE BLESSING

Blessed is the man or woman
Who spends time with You,
Praying to a living God
Who hears every thought,
Yet loves us as we are.

Blessed are we who know
The goodness that flows
From an everlasting Father
Who forgives our sins.

Blessed are the ones
Who call upon the Lord
For He shall answer them,
Even as they abide
Under the shelter of His wings.

Blessed are the children
Born not of the flesh but of spirit
For they shall know the secret place
Of the Most High.

Blessed are they who thirst for God
For there is no greater love.
Receive the blessings of a Father;
Receive the blessing of God.

David and me on our wedding day (April 5, 1986).

X

THE WILL OF GOD

And the world is passing away, and the lust of it,
but he who does the will of God abides forever

—1 JOHN 2:17

The will of God is a mystery to many. It took me years to get to where I trusted God with my life. After the pandemic started, there was a mass exodus from the workplace. I began to pray about the possibility of retirement. God began opening doors for my husband and me to retire, to my amazement. I had worked in the legal community for twenty-five years, and it was a big leap of faith to retire early. But I honestly felt God pulling me away from secular work. God's will is following the direction God is leading you. After many years of working full-time, I felt God pulling me toward writing. The blessing would later come through my husband's VA benefits, which would pay me to return to school. This actually supplemented my court retirement and made it so I could make more money staying home and going to school.

God has a destiny for you, it undoubtedly is different from mine but no less important. Not everyone is called away from secular work to focus on ministry and writing. But God's will for us does call us to a closer relationship with Him. The Bible says, "Oh, taste and see that the Lord is good; Blessed is the man who trusts in Him" (Psalms 34:8). You have nothing to lose and everything to gain. My prayer is that these poems will speak to you in a way that makes you realize that you are known and loved by God. There is power in prayer and walking with God. Take a few steps toward Him, and I promise He will meet your faith.

This is the final chapter of poems, but it contains some of the most important concepts in Christian life. That is following God's will for your life and fulfilling what God intended for you. We live in difficult times where prayer is not always honored by everyone, but it is necessary to follow God's will for your life. The letters Paul wrote in the epistles talk about the will of God, "For this reason, we also, since the day we heard it, do not cease to pray for you, and ask that you may be filled with the knowledge of His will in all wisdom and spiritual understanding" (Colossians 1:9). It takes work to pursue the will of God for your life. Paul also warned that we would need to step back from the ways of the world to pursue the perfect will of God, "And do not be conformed to this world, but be transformed by the renewing of your mind, that you may prove what that good and acceptable and perfect will of God" (Romans 12:2).

Most church people know these concepts, but my intention is to reach more than the people who already know Christ. Some have no idea what

I mean when I say "the will of God." But just as the scripture says, "seek, and you will find" (Matthew 7:7), if you are truly interested in knowing what God's will is for your life, seek God in prayer, and ask Him to reveal this to you. The Bible says, "Draw near to God, and He will draw near to you" (James 4:8). Those of you who have not known God in a personal way, I promise you, He will draw closer to you if you do this. If we only knew how much we are loved by God, we might see things differently. But since it is a personal walk of faith between you and God, you will have to decide for yourself. But just know this, if God has directed someone to share this book with you, there was a reason. This might be the first step of many to bring you into a relationship with God, my prayer is to provide some insight into this great mystery of knowing God and usher you into your own relationship with Him.

THE MASTER PLAN

When it seems life has no meaning,
You don't even understand.
When the puzzle seems so futile,
Put it in the Master's hands.

For there is no rhyme or reason
Why some things were meant to be,
But He knows the road your walking,
And He chose your destiny.

For the road that leads us upward
Often leads us through our trials,
But that road that seems so endless,
It will end in just a while.

So remember while you're walking,
There is One who walks with you.
His great love can heal your sorrow,
And His grace will see you through.

THE JOURNEY

Yesterday, forever gone
As memories still fade.
Cherished, yes, but soon forgotten,
Promises I've made.

I said that I would serve You, Lord,
But little did I know
That serving You was not enough,
But I must also grow.

Lord, help me to realize
My days here are so few.
When I suffer through a trial,
I'm suffering for You.

As I journey, I will face
More trials along the way,
But You're the God who walks with me.
You know the road I take.

FAITHFUL

Pieces of me seem to be
Scattered in the wind
By the storms of life,
But the glue that keeps
Me together …
Is God.

Heartache and loss,
Unanswered prayers,
Years of knowing Him
Have taught me
To trust in His will,
Realizing He knows
What tomorrow holds.
He has a plan …
For my life.

So today,
I give everything to Him,
Regardless of my feelings.
I honor Him with my life,
In good times and bad,
In abundance or not,
For He is always …
Faithful.

CLARITY

If only …
All of the little things
Made a difference,
But trying to stop the tide
Was a fruitless effort.
Enjoy the days of sunshine
And even the rain.
Life will go on,
And so will you.
Be grateful
For a moment of clarity
When you see the purpose
And the beauty of living.
Life is bittersweet,
Memories fade,
We can't change yesterday,
But we can enjoy today.

PERSPECTIVE

I sit here in silence,
Waiting to hear from You.
Waiting for the answer …
Why is there so much discord?
What is the solution?
I hear the voice of God.
You who stand in a congregation.
Where is the wisdom in allowing hatred
To influence our hearts and divide us?
Lord, where there is division,
Remind us that we are merely men,
Made a little lower than the angels,
We are all made in your image.
If we deny this, we deny our very existence.
Life is fragile, and hatred is cruel,
But God's mercies are new each day,
And from the perspective of heaven,
We were all made in the image of God.

THE CREATOR

The oceans roar Your praise.
That whisper in the breeze.
The mountains testify
Of greater things to see.

The love of God, so great
We cannot understand.
The God of all creation,
Has always had a plan.

The riches of His glory,
The treasure in our soul,
The never-ending story
That not too many know.

Lord, please give us wisdom
That we might understand
Your works within creation,
The gifts You gave to man.

Lead us to our calling
That is purely now our own
To create as our Creator.
To know as we are known.

Thank You, David,
For being a wonderful
Husband and best friend
And for your unwavering
Support for this
Book.

David and me.

9 781664 296596